50 Ways to Read Anyone, Anywhere, Anytime
Copyright ©2017 by Winson Tay

Notice of Rights

All rights reserved worldwide. No part of this publication may be reproduced, transmitted in any form or by any means, including photocopying, recording, stored in a retrieval system, or transmitted, in any form or any other electronic or mechanical methods, without the prior agreement and written permission of this author. Winson Tay is identified as the Author of this book and has been asserted in accordance with the Copyright, Designs and Patents Act 1988. All intellectual property rights written in this book belongs to Winson Tay. For permission requests, you can contact the author at the website below.

www.winsontay.com

Limit of Liability/Disclaimer of Warranty

The author has used his best efforts and resources in preparing this book, he makes no representations or warranties with respect to the accuracy or completeness of the contents of this book and specifically disclaim any implied warranties of merchantability or fitness for a particular purpose. No warranty may be created or extended by any sales representatives or written sales materials. The advice and strategies herein may not be suitable for your situation. You should consult with a professional where appropriate. Neither the publisher nor author shall be liable for any loss of profit or any other commercial damages, including but not limited to special, incidental, consequential, or other damages.

This book is published in a variety of electronic formats. Some content that appears in print may not be available in electronic books.

International ISBN: 978-981-11-3522-4
eBook ISBN: 978-981-11-3557-6

Written in Singapore. Printed in UK.
First Edition. 2017.

50

WAYS TO READ
ANYONE, ANYWHERE, ANYTIME

Publisher's Note

This publication contains the opinions and ideas of its author. It is intended to provide helpful and informative material on the subject matter covered. It is sold with the understanding that the author and publisher are not engaged in rendering professional services in this book. If the reader requires personal assistance or advice, a competent professional should be consulted.

The contents of this book should not be taken as financial advice, or as an offer to buy or sell any securities, fund, type of fund, or financial instruments. It should not be taken as an endorsement or recommendation of any particular company or individual, and no responsibility can be taken for inaccuracies, omissions, or errors. The information presented is not to be considered any investment advice. The reader should consult a registered investment advisor or registered dealer prior to making any investment decision.

The author does not assume any responsibility for actions or nonactions taken by people who have read this book, and no one shall be entitled to a claim for detrimental reliance based upon any information provided or expressed herein. Your use of any information provided here does not constitute any type of contractual relationship between yourself and the provider(s) of this information. The author hereby disclaims all responsibility and liability for all use of any information provided in this book.

The materials here are not to be interpreted as establishing an attorney-client relationship between the reader and the author of his firm. The views expressed herein are exclusively those of the author and do not represent the views of any other person or any organization with which the author may be associated.

This book is dedicated with love to:

My Grandma – Suzannah Ho

My Future Child

My Grandma,

You have guided me since the day I was born until I am ready to take on this world. Your unconditional love and support gives me enough power to move mountains. You are a dream come true for any grandchild in this entire universe. You are my best mentor.

My Future Child,

This book is for you. Your birth will be the greatest thing I will ever receive in years to come. You are my source for motivation, happiness, and fulfillment. You are the reason why I am pushing myself to my maximum potential every day, you are my shining light.

WHY YOU SHOULD OWN THIS BOOK

50 Ways to Read Anyone, Anywhere, Anytime is a book that will show you how to progress your life into the future. This book offers valuable insights on how to use Physiognomy to have an instant access to read anyone's face because they are open to anyone who knows how to read.

What if you could understand why a person behaves in a certain way just by looking at him or her? And why some people have successful businesses, good career progressions, and great relationships with their social circle?

What if you could solve any issues with your current or future spouse just by the revealing traits on their facial appearance? And what if you could discover your own authentic self to propel yourself to your passion of life? All of these could be achieved when you master the arts of Physiognomy.

Most people live their life by spending months or even years in trying to get to know someone. Only to realize that not everyone will stay with them for the rest of their lives. And therefore, they have to repeat the process all over again upon meeting someone new.

How many times can you sacrifice your time and repeat this process before meeting your desired friends who will stay with you for the rest of your life? Most people leave it to fate by placing bets on some random strangers in hope to meet their potential best friends or mentors.

This does not have to be the case when you truly understand the arts of Physiognomy. You will soon be able to learn about the different ways to decipher information about a person's personality, character, and their future pillars. If you want to have a better relationship with your spouse, social circles, and family, then this is the book for you.

We live in the present but we carry our concerns about the future or the past with us all the time. Let's be honest, we do wonder if we could change or transform our lives once in a while.

It does not matter if you have not considered to pick up this subject before, and it sure does not matter if you do not have any knowledge on how this is going to work. All that matter is, are you willing to take the dive to learn how to use this new skill and take advantage of it towards your favor. You can choose to provide this knowledge as a gift or wield it as a weapon. This will be a great source of information that I am going to offer to the world in years to come.

And here is what truly sets this book apart: I am going to share with you the strategies that the wealthy harness every day to improve their life. Why should the privileged few be the only ones to tap into extraordinary power? Isn't it time for us to level the playing field? Remember, your priceless gift of time belongs to you, and now it's time for you to take control.

About the Author

Author Winson Tay became dedicated to the idea of helping others discover their true passion of life ever since he embarked on his journey as a consultant. His life goal is to help others from all walks of life to take control of their destinies. In 2014, Physiognomy became his passion to understand how different facial features represent different meanings of life.

Having delivered numerous talks for banks and corporations, Winson used the aspects of Physiognomy, Ontology, Phrenology, and Cosmology to forecast their future growths and bring out the best employees in their industries.

These talks have inspired thousands of people to understand their life destinies through branches of face reading, four pillars of destiny, and positive programming. This in turn have produced massive results for their financial growth and unlocked their potential as a whole individual.

During the raw age of 22 when Winson first started, he faced numerous rejections as a young man without any client database. Today, he is sought after by a rapidly increasing pool of clientele for his professional consultancy and advice.

Most people think that Physiognomy is similar to fortune telling. Let us clarify this, Physiognomy does not define you have a permanently sad or happy life. Instead, Physiognomy is mostly used to forecast and show you how you can embrace your talents, and live your life to your maximum potential. You can choose to accept your forecasted scenarios, or you can decide to change them for the better.

Some people are lucky enough to have met their right mentors and unlocked their true potential early in life. The majority of people do not enjoy this privilege.

What if you could use this knowledge to look for the right mentors to assist you in your journey of life? And what if you could understand what abilities and talents you have, to put yourself on the path with the least resistance towards your success? This would mean that you will be able to do something you love and not feel aimless in life.

This is the reason why Winson wrote you this book. He wants to show you how to use Physiognomy to look for the right mentors, and to show you the light in discovering your passion.

If you have ever dreamt of achieving more and having more in your life, 50 Ways to Read Anyone, Anywhere, Anytime will show you how to get there.

If Winson has found that this worked at a very young age, he believes you can achieve similar success and even more. It is only a question of how.

Prologue

Take a moment to imagine a life where you can save the time in getting to know someone, and instead, spend those extra time in doing the things you love to do.

Imagine spending your time on building the right relationships with people who love you for who you truly are.

Imagine being able to discover your true passion in life and writing a letter to your boss that reads, "Thank you for everything boss, but from now onwards, I will be doing things that I truly love to do and live my life to my maximum potential."

Imagine living a meaningful life oriented to what you love based on your own nature and making a living from doing it.

All over the world now, thousands of people are rewriting their definition of work, they are becoming their own bosses by impacting our world in one way or another.

Every author, I suppose, will promise you massive results if you purchase their book. This book is different because it all boils down to you. How much you are willing to commit to yourself with what you are about to learn and take the necessary actions for the results to show.

Most people read a book with so much potential knowledge but they do not take any action. They just hope and assume that the knowledge will automatically be converted into actions in their own mind. This is not how it is supposed to be. You have to get out there and apply what you have learnt to source for the right people who will assist you in your journey of life.

This spontaneous search for solutions to decipher your own or other's destinies is a common trend for anyone in their own minds. This book is divided into two sections; Section 1 will cover on introduction, and Section 2 will cover on the arts of Face Reading.

You will be given a sense of complexity on how we can process our unconscious mind to construct a coherent interpretation of anyone in our world, at any instant. Your mind will soon be tuned to explain the heuristics of face reading and explore a major puzzle that the majority will never be able to decipher without this knowledge on their own.

My goal is to introduce you to a new way of thinking with your own mind that will be beneficial to you in years to come. There are no limitations in your mind as your potential is endless when you are equipped with the right tools and knowledge.

Contents

Why you should own this book	7
About the Author	9
Prologue	13
Section One: Introduction	21
Passion	24
Purpose	26
People and Partnerships	28
Two Ways to Read a Face	34
Changing Your Face	35
Achieving More	36
Two Ways to Use This Book	37
Section Two: Arts of Physiognomy	39
Foreheads:	
1 Flat Forehead	40
2 Angled Forehead	42
3 Bump Forehead	44
4 Wide Forehead	46
5 Narrow Forehead	48
Eyebrows:	
6 Line Eyebrows	50
7 Skinny Eyebrows	52

8	Happy Eyebrows	54
9	Leader Eyebrows	56
10	Full Eyebrows	58
11	Short Hair between Eyebrows	60
12	Wide Distance between Eyebrows	62
13	Narrow Distance between Eyebrows	64

Nose:

14	Huge Fleshy Nose	66
15	Tiny Nose	68
16	Downward Tip Nose	70
17	Upward Tip Nose	72
18	Long Lengthy Nose	74
19	Short Lengthy Nose	76
20	Pressed Protruding Nose	78
21	Primary Downward Nose	80

Ears:

22	Elevated Ears	82
23	Elevated Ears with Eye Types	84
24	Bottom Ears	86
25	Massive Ears	88
26	Mini Ears	90
27	Circular Ears	92
28	Types of Helix Ears	94
29	Types of Earlobes	96
30	Long Earlobes	98

Eyes:

31	Our Eyes	100
32	Massive Eyes	102
33	Mini Eyes	104
34	Circular Eyes	106
35	Narrow Set of Eyes	108

36	Wide Set of Eyes	110
37	Embedded Eyes	112
38	Popping Eyes	114
39	Upward Set Eyes	116
40	Downward Set Eyes	118
41	Special Effects for Eyes	120

Lips:

42	Massive Lips	122
43	Mini Lips	124
44	Upward Lip Line	126
45	Downward Lip Line	128
46	Straight Lip Line	130

Chin:

47	Circular Chin	132
48	Squarish Chin	134
49	Arrow Chin	136
50	Popping Chin	138

| Acknowledgements | 141 |

| Bonuses for you | 151 |

A better world is when people with more information can conquer their priceless gift, which is the gift of life.

-Winson Tay

SECTION ONE

INTRODUCTION

So what is Physiognomy all about?

It's simply a tool, a source of power used in service for others and is intensely personal and highly charged. Physiognomy is about gathering insights about a person, just by looking at their facial features. It is a fascinating technique for anyone to know about a person's personality traits, attitudes, health conditions, as well as fate if you believe in it! It is vital and crucial, but not paramount.

To get you started, this book will show you how to read anyone with certain facial features, and hence understand them as a whole individual. There are more than a thousand ways to read anyone in existence and the following ways will be ready in years to come.

Physiognomy is mostly used to discover your passions that are yet to be developed. Most of my clients have the tendency to assume that the rewards will automatically show itself after they have found the route to their passion. This is not the case!

You have to grind and work on your talents for them to show their maximum potential for results. You have to take time to practice and hone your skills over and over again by putting yourself in the right place where you can generate the most returns for your own success.

It is not only about becoming good in your skills, you have to become great in what you do. If you want to achieve the most out of your life, you have to be perfectly great in showcasing your talents and skills.

When you acquire and master your skill sets, it becomes easier for you to move up the corporate ladder, and expand your capacity to generate wealth. If you do not do anything to discover your true passion of life, would you agree that it is a complete waste of your presence in this universe?

We are all born with special talents to offer to this world and I would say that it is our responsibility to discover what they are.

After working with corporations and start-ups for years, I know, of course, there are so many factors that influence the success of any venture.

There are multiple factors, like environmental, resources, appropriate business partners, the niche of your product, and the list goes on. What I am offering here is something which falls into the category that most people deemed it as luck.

Most of the time, an entrepreneur cannot control this factor because they are not exposed on how to use Physiognomy towards their favor. Despite if he or she needs to consider them, they will simply pay the price for not knowing how to use it.

We all want to leave a legacy or perhaps our own footprint in this world. And to do that, we need to create something of value that will in turn help enrich lives. My mentor always says: "Don't try to change the world. Discover your purpose, serve others well, and the world will change around you."

Passion

All great achievements begin with passion. Passion is what fuels your drive to get things done. Passion is what motivates you every day and shapes your purpose in life. If you rally around your purpose and reinvent your own culture around it, you will meet success. If you don't, you will meet failure.

The lesson here? Every entrepreneur is not afraid to use any inspiration that comes his way and use them with pride. Some of the most successful people today see the need to identify what is lacking and offered a product or service to bridge that gap.

They see the opportunity to do something better and committed themselves to doing it. But they execute it with their own originality by utilizing their knowledge and experience they have gathered over the years to create something special.

It does not matter where your inspirations or ideas come from. Your ideas may not be completely original, but always execute your masterpiece with authenticity fueled by your passion.

Your passion fuels your success. No doubt. Several extraordinary people have proven this formula. But I would like to emphasize on another crucial factor shared by every entrepreneur who have achieved success out there: the ability to take action!

Without acting on it, your desire is just a desire. Nothing will come out of a desire if you don't take any action and work on it. This is what separates great entrepreneurs from the good ones: they act and not only plan.

I have full certainty to say that one does not have to be a genius to create something extraordinary to impact our world. In today's century, the average people are the ones who spearhead true change.

They do not come from wealthy backgrounds or they might not be a graduate from the top universities in the world. And that is they are willing to take massive action on their desires to work on their passion.

They are willing to risk everything they have, by failing, and getting up to try again. This is how passion serves as a catalyst to fuel your burning desire to the execution of your ideas.

Passion ignites us, motivates us, and assists us to persevere through any challenges. If you have achieved some success today, you will realize that passion is one of your key ingredients for success.

Your passion is what helps you to understand who you are and what you want to accomplish out of your life. This understanding shapes your life purpose and this purpose is how you craft your ideas, creations, mold your products, and deliver your innovation.

Purpose

Any business with a clear purpose will tell you why a company exists. Great companies are able to share with you what they stand for and what they believe in. They want people to matter. And this sense of purpose, of belonging, of we are a family is a feeling that inspire others.

Everything a successful company does starts from its purpose. Be it from the products it manufactures, the employees they hire, the working environment they offer, the partnerships they have, the investors they attract, the way they market their products, and the way they deliver customer service.

The reality in today's world is that any products or services can be easily copied by your competitors. But what really breeds long-term customer loyalty and the success of any company is the belief your customers have towards your company.

When the purpose of your company is to focus on serving others in life, your employees and customers will be willing to stand next to you in the execution of this purpose.

Purpose is essential to determine the success of any endeavor. Purpose is the key to give companies true authenticity. And with Physiognomy, you will be able to discover your passion or your purpose towards anything in life!

Like I have said earlier, I've personally worked with many businesses throughout my career, and I have seen so many brilliant people come up with fantastic ideas that are bound to have golden opportunities. But most of the ideas were not executed due to the lack of passion and courage to turn those ideas into a reality.

To be completely honest, I have also seen average people who have minimal resources, education, and experience they require into creating a successful venture. But they are so dedicated to their dreams that it is almost impossible for them to not create any masterpiece.

No doubt they have failed numerous times, but they continued to redefine their ideas and stay true to their passion until they succeed. What I am saying is, those who are passionate enough to pioneer your dreams will make them happen eventually!

The successful execution for your passion will depend on your current environment and several external factors. Physiognomy is one of the major key external factors to assist you in achieving your success in ways you can ever imagine.

People and Partnerships

I believe the two key factors to make an impact for any successful company is: its people and partnerships.

Having the right or wrong candidates on board will determine the success of any business venture. And to align it with the right partners is a critical decision for any entrepreneurs who would like to set out on their own. By using Physiognomy, you could minimize the damages and losses should the business venture head south.

There is no more vital factor in the long run success of any company than the quality of its own human capital. There are so many books that have touched on the importance of having a good team.

Whether you are in the midst of growing your business or you already have an established one, if your team does not share your vision, mission, and your goals of the company, your business will never be able to reach its full potential.

No matter how brilliant your ideas are, success requires team work. You can imagine the most amazing ideas in the world, but you require the right people to turn those dreams into a reality. For any endeavor to be successful, you need a team of people who shares your company's vision. This vision is commonly known as the purpose for existence.

To a certain extent, people can be intelligent, or have special skill sets which are applicable to your business. But if they don't believe in their own maximum potential, they are not going to give it their all.

The right candidates are not those who have the right competency, they are the ones who have the right attitude in growing your company. There are some successful companies which I have worked with, adopted the approach of hiring the best talents first and then worry about choosing the right roles for them.

There is nothing wrong with this approach. But what if there is a way to help you understand all your candidates before you even get started, would you use it?

Value your employees by their value-based behaviors or what their maximum potential capabilities are, and not by their age or credentials. Always hire for their attitude. Skills can be taught, but their own burning desire towards your company can never be taught.

Your people are your own brand. Each one of your employees is your brand's face, your brand's ambassador, and your brand's marketer. The secret to successful hiring is to look for people who wants to impact the world with your brand! And how do you discover that? Physiognomy!

You could also develop smart hiring strategies to stay consistent with your cultural values by bringing the right partnerships and people on board with Physiognomy!

Great companies that are founded are never done by one person; they are accomplished by a team of people. Partners have to complement each other very well to co-create.

True collaboration is a powerful thing. When partners are able to share their ideas with like-minded people, they are able to look for different angles to execute and shape their ideas for the better. What is better is, it allows them to turn those ideas into a reality.

As cliché as this may sound, a partnership is like a yin and yang. You need to have both partners who have different personalities but are able to work well together. You do not want to have two very peaceful or two blazing personalities in a partnership.

This will not only balance out the way on how you hire and treat your employees, but this will also balance out the strategies your partnership might execute for your potential clients.

Business partners can either be your greatest asset, or they can be your biggest nightmare for your business.

On one hand, a partner can have the capability to provide you with their own diversity in skills, financial resources, and even new network opportunities.

However, on the other hand, a partner can give you the lack of commitment, a complicated relationship, or get you into legal and financial disputes.

Now, don't jump into the conclusion that we are stereotyping individuals with Physiognomy here. We are merely understanding why some people behave in a certain manner according to their different facial shapes, trends, and structures.

Let's keep an open mind. I know some of you are already satisfied with your life. Most of my clients have decided to stick to their day jobs because they are satisfied with how they are doing. However, there are also some of them who do not know whether they should continue with their current jobs or change for a better one.

Here is my take. If you are satisfied with your life, what is stopping you from becoming the best in what you do? What is stopping you from becoming five or probably 10 times better? If you are telling me you are doing fine now, I believe you can do even better in 10 years!

The question is, have you positioned yourself to embrace your full potential and showcase your talents?

If you have, maybe you can achieve more without taking the leap. But if you have not, what have you been doing with your life?

You might say you do not want to risk everything in your life right now. That is fine, but the problem is, our world is changing rapidly, and our economy is growing at a much faster pace than your paycheck.

Soon enough, our world will outgrow you and what might seem normal to you now, will not be the same in the future. Therefore, I would say, keep moving forward and make all the constant progress in your life!

If this have worked for thousands of people and resolved countless of personal and work issues, I do not see how this is not going to work for you if you use Physiognomy right.

You can use this knowledge to focus on all your strengths and improve yourself as a person, or you could use this to understand your superiors, and increase your probability of getting a promotion.

Can you imagine how much time and money you could save by leveraging on this helpful and yet simple knowledge? I hope that when you are done with this book, you will be able to decipher several traits of a person just by taking a glance at them.

To decipher each feature, you have to learn how to recognize the different trends of facial features and understand the meaning of each of their corresponding personality traits.

In order to make the best out of face reading, you must be able to decipher separate facial features together instead of just looking at one facial feature alone.

Would you be able to answer if I ask you questions like, "how wide are your eyes apart?", "Is your nose the same length as your ears?", and "How is your chin sloped to your mouth?"

You will be surprised if I tell you that most people will look at me in daze when these questions are thrown at them. Some will probably take out their camera phones to have a look at their own facial features.

In the past, you need to know the answers to learn Face Reading. But today, I have made this subject so easy for you by writing this book. All you need to do now is to take a look at the images or search for the relevant examples I have provided for you to do face reading. I promise you, the more you practice this, the better you will become.

TWO WAYS TO READ A FACE

The first way to read a face is known as "fixed position face reading."

This is done by reading a feature on a face to reveal a certain attribute. Simply said, one feature defines one attribute. For example, if someone who has a large nose without any sight of nostrils, defines he or she has a huge potential for their accumulation of wealth.

The second way to read a face is known as "several position face reading."

This refers to several readings of facial features on a face to form an outcome. Various facial features will be evaluated like understanding the attributes of a fleshy nose, crystal clear eyes, and strong laughter lines to decipher how much potential streams of income a person can work on for accumulating wealth.

We will be covering on both ways to read a face in this book to give you a comprehensive understanding on how this can be done. You will soon be able to understand how the facial features are distinctly shaped to define their corresponding traits.

CHANGING YOUR FACE

The most frequent question that always pops up when I am giving a talk is, "Would going for a cosmetic surgery changes my wellbeing as a person?"

The answer is "YES! And it has always been yes!" When you go for a cosmetic surgery to change the structures of your face, it will affect and alter your life when you are done with it.

WHY?

After the completion of a surgery, the surgery is going to change the way you look and feel about yourself. When you have new perceptions about yourself, are you going to behave and approach others differently? YES!

This would result your family and social circles to look at you in a different way. So the school of thought is, to always change your facial features that is resonated with better attributes. If you insist to go for a complete makeover of your face, at least know what you are getting yourself into.

ACHIEVING MORE

Most people have gambled their life away by leaving their life journey to fate.

They think that if they can increase the amount of people they meet, they will eventually meet their life benefactors. It may be true, but won't this lead them to spending more time to get to know them as a person?

Life can be far more predictable, and far more profitable if you live life by taking the right actions. People who have achieved certain status in life are mainly due to the information they are being exposed to.

Now, think about your role model or someone you aspire to be. Would you agree that they are being exposed to certain information, and they took the right actions to get to where they are today? This tells you if you immerse yourself with the same information and take the right actions, you can achieve similar results.

If you are tired of throwing yourself rapidly outside with a random chance, allow me to teach you a technique by using Physiognomy to get more outcome with least effort.

TWO WAYS TO USE THIS BOOK

You can read this book on your own or you could read it with a group of people to learn face reading by doing it on each other.

On your own

Read this book straight from the start and pay close attention to how the facial features are formed, by understanding the representations behind each facial feature. You can create a self-study plan by starting to memorize the different foreheads first, before moving down to the different eyebrows and so on.

Ensure that you understand the associated features and how you can apply this into any part of your life. With this approach, you will learn to better relate to all sorts of people and make progress in your leadership and personal abilities.

With a group

Gather a group of your colleagues or social circle to go through this book together. Discuss the attributes for each of the facial features and help one another out by applying the insights discussed in this book. It will be a lot more enjoyable if you could do it on each other to learn faster with the examples provided.

I hope someday all educational and corporations will use Physiognomy as a guide to get to know one another. For now, you have an edge among them.

Are you ready to take the dive and change the way you look at this world? The knowledge you are about to discover will allow you to make all the right decisions quickly while enjoying the moments of a happy and successful future. You are about to be blown away on what you are going to discover. Shall we begin?

SECTION TWO

ARTS OF PHYSIOGNOMY (FACE READING)

1

Flat Forehead

A Flat Forehead denotes a person who is a progressive thinker. This person thinks and complete their tasks in a systematic manner. An example would be having a list to do things. They have the mindset of completing the first task before moving on to the second task and so on.

Their peers might laugh at them for living their lives by the book. But in fact, they are very intelligent people who are cautious in what they do. Their progressive style of thinking is perfect for being analyzers or managers to keep a company moving.

People with a Flat Forehead tend to face problems especially when they are under pressure. For example, when they must complete certain tasks within a time limit. Reason being, they require more time to think progressively for better results. Therefore, if you have colleagues with Flat Foreheads, do not give them too much pressure. Give them sufficient space for them to work, and you will get the best quality out of their work.

2

Angled Forehead

People with an Angled Forehead are known to be quick responders. They are constantly on the move due to their natural behavior of being quick-witted. They enjoy living their life on a fast-paced basis, and they have the tendency of guessing what you are about to say next. Hence, they will always create their own conclusion for answers at the back of their heads.

Occasionally, they may interrupt you while in the midst of having a conversation with them. To the certain extent where you may find them relatively rude and ill-mannered. This is the reason why there is a high possibility of them being unentertained when they speak to the majority of people who fail to keep up with their pace.

If you look at most professional athletes, you will notice that most of their foreheads are slopped this way as they are always on the move. Their core strength is known to be quick decision-makers despite any situation. Sometimes this may lead them to many problems in the long run due to their tendency of acting first without evaluating the consequences.

3

Bump Forehead

People with a Bump Forehead are known to be creative with their thoughts, as they mostly excel in arts, design, or performing arts. When you take a close look at those who do well in fine arts, you will see that most of them have this feature.

Their creative caps are beyond extraordinary, as they have amazing imaginations to think outside the box. If you have any colleagues who have this feature, do not give them any task which is based on numbers. They tend to sabotage themselves whenever numbers come into the picture. It's not that they are not fond of numbers; their mistakes with them are bound to happen! Furthermore, do not give them specific orders to follow or have any restrictions to what they can contribute. Give them some personal space and you will see that they will excel in many ways.

If their forehead is curved with more than 70% on their face, this means that the person is very intelligent and will always give you plenty of creative solutions to any questions for the problems you ask.

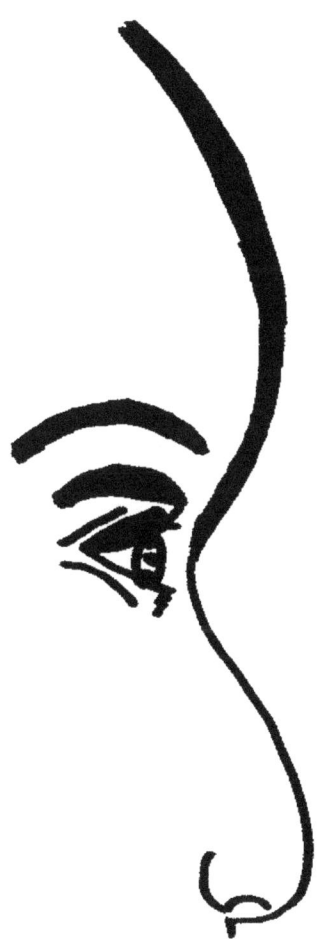

4

Wide Forehead

A Wide Forehead denotes intelligence and is known to be a very good facial feature to have. This is derived when you could fit 5 or more of your fingers on your forehead starting from the top of their eyebrows to your hairline. If you are bald, you can estimate this with your hairline to do this evaluation. People with Wide Foreheads are known to be very intelligent or even genius in their wildest ideas.

If you take a look at the rich and powerful people in the world, you will see that most billionaires or business leaders are bound to have this facial feature. People with a Wide Forehead are great public speakers, presenters, business owners, and generally high flyers in their own fields. They simply take control of their life by giving orders to others.

If you have this facial feature, you should contribute something to this world as you have the potential to create a service or a product that could impact our world greatly. Examples of business leaders who have this facial feature would be Warren Buffett, and Hong Kong tycoon, Li Ka-Shing.

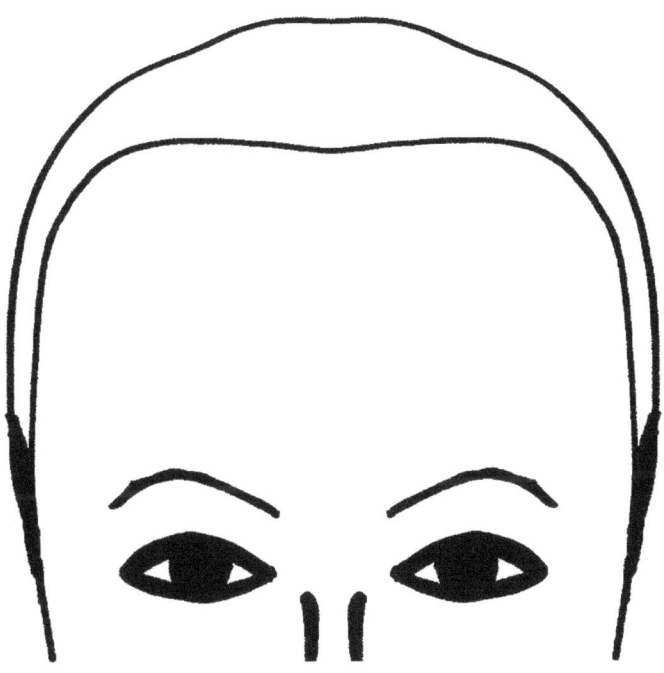

5

Narrow Forehead

A Narrow Forehead is derived from fitting 4 or less of your fingers starting from the top of your eyebrows to your hairline. If you are bald, you can estimate this with your hairline to do this evaluation. People with a Narrow Forehead are known to be logical thinkers, and they can be very theoretical in the way they speak.

They make great system managers, as they are more suited to have a system to follow and execute their talents. When they have found a role model to look up to as an icon, it becomes easier for them to achieve their desired success of life. Simply said, they need to be inspired, to be aspired by others. They may face difficulties in brainstorming for new ideas, as their creative caps is quite limited for ideas to flow. Unless they are exposed to a wide range of unimaginative knowledge. They should work on this aspect to increase their potential for greatness.

In some cases, some people will have a combination of two forehead profiles. For example, a slightly angled, and narrow forehead. When they have these two facial features, they will possess the traits of both features and the combination of both attributes that is associated.

6

Line Eyebrows

People with Line Eyebrows are commonly seen to be set as straight lines. They are known to be logical, ambitious, and business-minded. They are constantly on the move to meet new people to grow their networks at social events.

However, they can appear cold and unaffectionate to others as they hardly show any emotions. Primarily, they do not allow their emotions to come into the process for their decision making. When you are having business dealings with them, you are encouraged to show them evidence by using papers that are well drafted out to show them the desired outcome. People with Line Eyebrows can only make their decisions when they are truly convinced by what you are offering after seeing it on paper.

Nonetheless, they are good friends to talk to when you are facing any personal issues. They are great problem solvers, and they can give you insights to understand the root of the problem.

7

Skinny Eyebrows

People with Skinny Eyebrows are seen to be very thin on their face. They are very emotional, yet good looking people on the outside. However, they are highly sensitive at how others look at them. They are constantly thinking about how they are being portrayed in the minds of others. Despite allowing their emotions for decision making, this can lead them to unwanted conflicts between their social circle and family.

If you know someone who have these eyebrows, they must be appreciated for what they have done for others. You are encouraged to show them appreciation and give in to them to make the best out of your relationship. Bear in mind that they do not handle critics well, and harmful words may lead them to do foolish things as a result.

When the strands of the hair are going both upwards and downwards throughout the entire shape of their eyebrows, be extra careful as they are incredibly sensitive to any words you say.

8

Happy Eyebrows

People with Happy Eyebrows are seen to be cheerful, and have an approachable persona in them. They are projected to be gentle, considerate, and well-balanced people. They love to put others before themselves, to be surrounded with positive energy. When you see people with Happy Eyebrows, they tend to boost up your day one way or another.

If you are trying to convince someone with these eyebrows, the best way for you to convince them is to use different scenarios and metaphors. This will put them into the storyline for them to get a grip on the illustration you are sharing.

To understand their thoughts, place yourself in their shoes, and you will be able to understand how they think, analyze, and evaluate to make their final decision. Generally, they are the ones who are easier to convince for any business dealings. Now you know who you should focus on when meeting business clients!

9

Leader Eyebrows

Leader Eyebrows can be seen when it is flipped like a reverse V as seen on the right. They have a strong willpower to get things done to make a difference. They can be very nasty when it comes to work, as they are highly motivated and will never settle for anything that is ordinary. Simply said, they dislike doing tasks for average results!

They are constantly on the move for popularity, status, power, fame, and recognition in their own field of work. They demand high status of respect in their workplace, and they love to be the limelight when everyone is focused on them.

As they are results oriented, they can sometimes appear to be too controlling to their employees and even to their own spouse. They have a high tendency to slowly lose interest in their passion, hobbies, and their own love life over a period of time. Take a look at most business leaders and you will see that most of them have this feature.

10

Full Eyebrows

People with Full Eyebrows can be seen when the eyebrows are connected from one point to the other without a breaking gap in between. This is a very unfavorable eyebrow to have, as it denotes plenty of unfavorable attributes. You are strongly encouraged to change and trim this eyebrow of yours if it is possible.

They are known to be very stingy, and failing to place others before themselves. Thus, their friends will be negatively affected in the long run, as they see themselves in the losing end of the relationship. People with Full Eyebrows are also known to be very calculative people who will count every debt to the very cent. An example would be, if you borrowed $22.80 from them, they will take nothing less than that amount. In extreme cases, they will hold grudges against you, and plan to get back at you with the mindset of you cheating them.

They have a high tendency to overthink every possible scenario and they commonly face loss of sleep. They simply need to relax their mind so that their health will not be affected. If you know someone who have these eyebrows, accept them for who they are and don't walk away from them for having all these negative attributes.

11

Short Hair between Eyebrows

When you look closely at someone who have short strands of hair growing between their eyebrows, they can be very conservative people who will seldom start any conversation. They are deemed to be introverts by nature, but they will give you the impression of being extroverts on the outside. They are also known to be very selective in deciding which product to pick before making any purchase.

They can be quite calculative at times, but not to the extent of someone with Full Eyebrows. For example, they will remember who owes them money, but have a minimal tendency of making a scene out of it. In extreme cases, they might ask you for some of the amount back to strike you off in their minds. They are harmless compared to people with Full Eyebrows, as they are less likely to hurt others when they are offended.

To understand further if a person is a giver or a taker in terms of their facial features, take a look at 12 & 13 for the gap distance between their eyebrows to see how this would affect them as individuals.

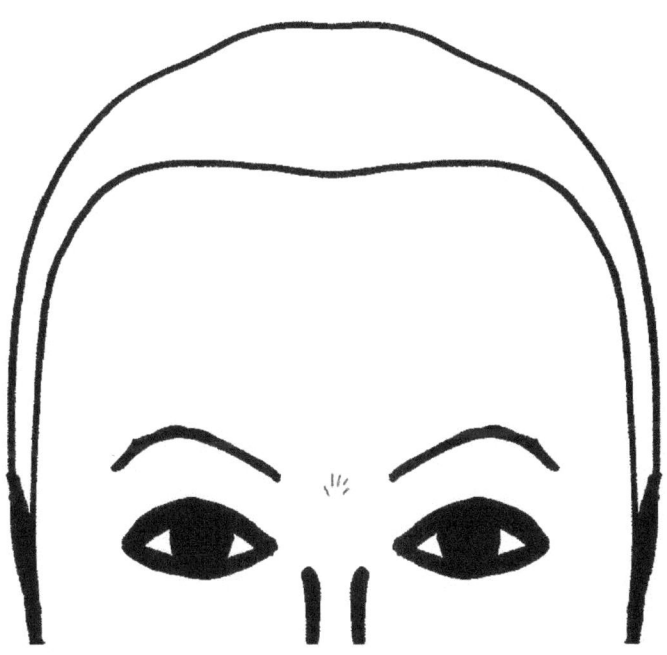

12

Wide Distance between Eyebrows

To determine if someone has a Wide Distance between their Eyebrows, they will need to be able to place two and a half fingers in between them. They are known to be exceptionally generous to their social circle, and will shower them with plenty of gifts. This is one of the primary reasons why they are well loved by others.

They simply have the mindset of giving others first before receiving any gifts. With them around, you will have the luxury to receive anything from them. What's even better is, they do not expect to receive any from you in return! They are so generous that they will always buy you meals when you dine with them.

Should they receive any gifts from you, they will remember you for it and return you with more gifts you could possibly imagine. In summary, they will always give more than they will receive over the long run. You could try and hint them the list of things you'd love to have, and who knows? They might just get it for you!

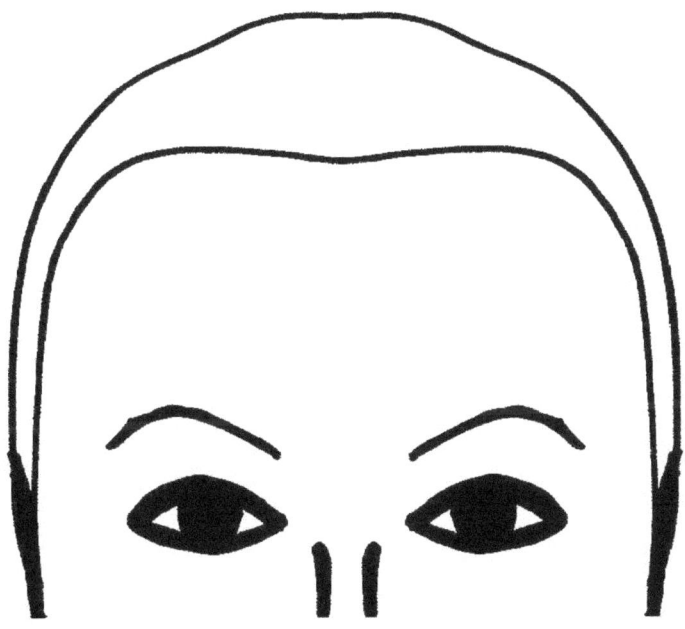

13

Narrow Distance between Eyebrows

Narrow Distance between Eyebrows is a result of not being able to fit two fingers in between your eyebrows. They tend to have the mindset of receiving first before giving. They look forward to receiving gifts from others, but they are not willing to flood gifts to others around them. They simply have a different perception for networking.

They will constantly have thoughts and doubts, as to why they should be giving gifts to others. People with Narrow Distance between Eyebrows do not see the benefits of giving. Therefore, they tend to be more selfish in nature, as they have the mindset of the world revolving around them. Sometimes, they might even deliberately take their time to retrieve their wallets in hoping that their friends will settle the bill for them.

This in turn might cause their social circle to feel that they are being taken advantage, and hence causing them to distant themselves away. If the distance between your eyebrows fits two fingers perfectly, you're considered to be a neutral individual, which is in the middle of these two attributes.

14

Huge Fleshy Nose

People with a Huge Fleshy Nose are seen to have wider nose tips and longer nose bridges. They lead a better quality of life, as they have the capacity to generate plenty of wealth making ideas. This favorable nose represents their ability to create both primary and passive income easily when they discover their talents in life. Their earning power are beyond imaginable!

However, they dislike receiving orders from superiors and enjoy being their own boss. They love to give orders to others, as they are constantly focusing on growing their own company. Thus, they do not spend much time doing and working on the smaller tasks that do not benefit them in the long run.

This is why most people who have this nose are business owners and high ranking officials, as they tend to chase for higher status in life. They tend to provide massive value to the community and this is why they are always seen as an icon among others. A perfect example of someone who has this facial feature would be Hollywood action star, Jackie Chan.

15

Tiny Nose

People with a Tiny Nose are seen to have smaller nose tips and shorter nose bridges. Generally, they have lesser earning power than the majority, as the feature of a nose represents the capacity to generate wealth. But nonetheless, they are very reliable people. People with such feature are mostly found to be the best personal assistants in the world, as they love dealing with systematic and repetitive work.

They are great problem solvers and they love to handle any problems that are related to their job. They love to do their work process all over again, as they see themselves as someone who have the determination and perseverance to repeat the same process.

Despite providing so much value to their superiors, their pay increments can be generally slow unless they are on good terms with their bosses. If you have employees who have this feature, you can certainly give them the things you dislike to do. They are one of the most reliant people you can count on to get the job done. Do remember to reward them well if they are giving you massive value, or they will look for someone else who will appreciate their worth.

16

Downward Tip Nose

People with a Downward Tip Nose will give you the impression of an eagle's beak when you look at them from the side. They are constantly surrounded with plenty of opportunities and benefactors who are willing to help them. This is why they tend to receive promotions quicker compared to others and would eventually result them in having a higher primary income.

At times, they can be manipulative, and exaggerate situations with false information to trick others into believing their own story. They possess an egoistic nature, as they crave for the public's attention to recognize them as a highly respected, and reputable figure.

If you look at Hollywood entertainment industry, most international celebrities have this facial feature, and are well respected by millions of people. An example for someone who has this facial feature would be Microsoft Founder, Bill Gates.

17

Upward Tip Nose

People with an Upward Tip Nose can be seen when their nose tips are pointing towards the sky. They are one of the most gullible people around, why? They simply trust every word that is thrown to them.

When their nostrils are revealed together, they are quite the spendthrift towards their wealth. They will spend a hefty amount on others to make their social circle happy. They believe that the finer things are the joy in life. With the lack of financial discipline, they tend to spend every dollar they make. Their indulgence for entertainment, luxury goods, and better quality food is something they desire.

They also have a high tendency to be cheated by others for business ventures, as they have the mindset that the world is filled with good people. If you have friends with this facial feature, give them a slight warning, and do not attempt to cheat their savings away!

18

Long Lengthy Nose

People with a Long Lengthy Nose is derived from having long nose bridges that will stretch at least one third in length on their face. They generally have good business sense to run profitable businesses.

They have the greatest instincts to forecast business growths, and have a strong sense of ambition to break the status quo. When they are faced with any obstacles or issues, they can muster all of their courage to solve any problems.

When their nose tip is seen to be bulbous, every business they get into are money-making machine. Their businesses are going to run without their presence in the company, and their social circle will always envy their growth in career. That is, when there are no birth marks, moles, or scars on their nose. Without any of these signs, this is a very favorable nose to have if you want to be a business leader.

19

Short Lengthy Nose

People with a Short Lengthy Nose can be seen when they have short nose bridges. They are very emotional and sensitive people. At times, they can be over-protective about themselves. Despite being carefree people, they need to be constantly motivated as they are very skilled and proficient with plenty of skills under their belt.

You will not know how many special skills they have until they decide to reveal all of them to you. They also have the ability to adapt themselves quickly into any environment without affecting their quality of work.

On the downside, they might need to work on their leadership quality. They tend to be intimidated and shy away when they see their superiors or colleagues possessing strong leadership quality. If their middle nose tip is pointing downwards like an eagle's beak, they have tremendous potential to be very successful in their ventures, and loyalty is a must to their business partners. An example of such a self-made entrepreneur would be Alibaba founder, Jack Ma.

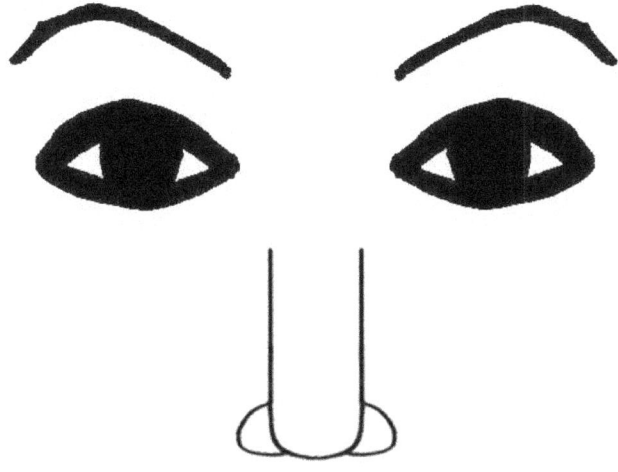

20

Pressed Protruding Nose

A Pressed Protruding Nose is a common yet unusual nose to have, but it denotes positive attributes. This nose is slightly pressed inwards throughout the middle part of the nose, and ending off with a pointy nose tip that is protruding outwards.

Marilyn Monroe is a perfect example for someone who has this nose. The bulky and fleshy tip is the icon of how a pressed protruding nose is formed. People with this nose are usually easy to approach at social events. They are optimistic in their own thoughts, and love to look at things from an optimistic standpoint. They tend to focus on all the positive outcome that can happen in their life.

If you need assistance from others, approach them! They are very open in supporting others should they need their help. Especially, when someone who is dear to them is struggling with finances. However, their sexual drive can be relatively high, and they can be very adventurous with their partner in their private life.

21

Primary Downward Nose

A Primary Downward Nose is seen from the obvious dent in the middle of the nose bridge. This nose tip is protruding downwards while the side bridges are going upwards. People with this nose have an unbeatable character, who tends to portray their love for music with a kind demeanor.

They are very pleasing people who will constantly show love towards their family and friends. Their special talents would be performing arts, as the movements they portray are a comforting sight for others to see. If you have this nose, you should work on public speaking, or theatre arts to unlock your full potential.

However, people with this nose are highly uncontrolled towards their sexual fantasies, and could end up cheating on their spouse and regret it later on. Reason is, they value the relationship with their partner, but they could have done so in a moment of lust. Therefore, take note of this aspect and you could minimize the possibility of this from happening. An example of someone who has this facial feature would be Hollywood Actor, Zac Efron.

22

Elevated Ears

Elevated Ears are seen to be high positioned and will attract your attention whenever you see them. This beautiful feature is always set higher than the eyebrows. This denotes that the person is very bright, and have the capacity to acquire high academic potential for scholarly results.

They tend to focus plenty of time on getting their job done, instead of looking for ways to get them done. When they are given new information, they usually absorb it much faster than others. You will see them shine especially when they are under pressure, as they tend to show more results when there is a deadline in play. Simply said, they love working in an intense environment.

They have the nature of taking their time to consider their options while shopping at a store, and this will always drive the salespeople insane. They tend to ask too many questions for comparisons to get the best purchase. Therefore, this made them to be very practical, and they will never make a purchase if they do not need the product.

23

Elevated Ears with Eye Types

To understand how people with Elevated Ears think and operate their mind, we look further into how they process their speed of information due to their eye features.

People with Elevated Ears with the combination of Huge Eyes will face difficulties when they are thrown with an overwhelming load of information. They tend to face issues when they are flooded with information, as they suffer from the ability to process them. Thus, this makes them frustrated when they are put in a fast-paced environment.

People with Elevated Ears with the combination of Mini Eyes are able to multitask efficiently, as they can process their incoming information quickly like a satellite system. As a result, when they are put under pressure, they tend to make better decisions compared to other Elevated Ears combination.

24

Bottom Ears

Bottom Ears are seen to be positioned below the eyebrow level when seen from the side. They love to move in slower paces and they prefer to do things one at a time. Bottom Ears are known to have a slower rate for receiving and processing any incoming information. If you are giving them quick instructions to follow, they will be lost with your words and hence, losing you in the process.

Nonetheless, they are idealistic people who have the ability to focus on how to get the job done instead of just getting it done. Therefore, if you are giving them any instructions, ensure that you provide them slowly by giving them diagrams and pictures for them to get a better understanding.

An interesting combination to look out for: when you see people who have Huge Eyes with Bottom Ears, they are commonly the last ones to complete their projects, as it is their nature to do things slowly and efficiently.

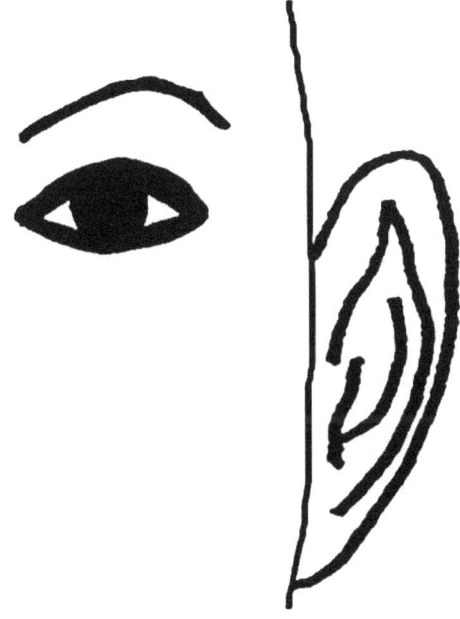

25

Massive Ears

Massive Ears can be seen when someone who have exceptionally large ears. They are very lively people and have an energetic persona to listen to any stories you tell them. They are the ones you can turn to whenever you need a listening ear to share your life events and stories.

This is a favorable ear to have because it represents the ability to be a sponge for information. People with Massive Ears generally have a happier childhood because their parents will support them with everything they want to do. These ears are also a great representation of vitality and longevity. If you look at most old aged people, you will notice that they have extremely Massive Ears!

The downside for Massive Ears would be the ability of exposing to unnecessary information from negative people. If you belong to this group of people, and you mix yourself with the wrong peers, you will absorb all of their problems into your life quicker than you can imagine. And this could be detrimental to your own success! So, choose your social circle wisely!

26

Mini Ears

People with Mini Ears are seen to have very small ears. Due to their nature of filtering incoming information, they are very cautious in listening to what others have to say. In some cases, they can be exceedingly rebellious and value friendships over their own family members.

They are prone to listening to their own inner voice and only to people whom they deem is right to hear. Due to their own nature, they have an inner ego whereby they feel that they are smarter than others. Generally, they lack the ability to learn from others and this might be their biggest disadvantage for them to grow as a person.

But fret not; if you belong to this group of people, I encourage you to be more open to listening only to your right mentors. If you can absorb and focus on all the right information, you can turn your disadvantage into your biggest advantage and propel yourself to success. This is how you use Physiognomy to your advantage!

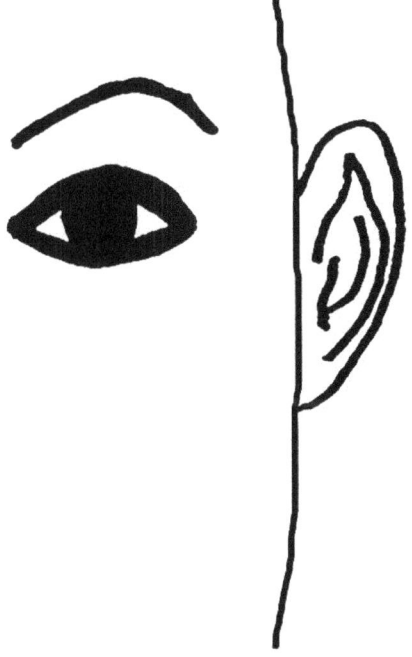

27

Circular Ears

Circular Ears are seen to be rounded when you look at them from the front, as shown on the right in the diagram. They are immensely positive, and imaginative with their own thoughts on a daily basis. They will seize all the limelight at social events, due to their nature of being incredibly outgoing with strangers.

When you need something to be done privately without anyone knowing, they are one of the most reliable people you can count on to get it done. If their ears are sticking outwards in full view as seen on the right, they are very independent people, but can be stubborn at times. Nonetheless, they project an incredible strong personality of independence.

If you have any friends who have these ears, stick close to them! They tend to attract plenty of money-making opportunities. Despite so, they are very mysterious people, and secretive deep down in their hearts. In special cases, if the top of their ears is pointed upwards like a pixie, they could talk their way out to get anything to come their way.

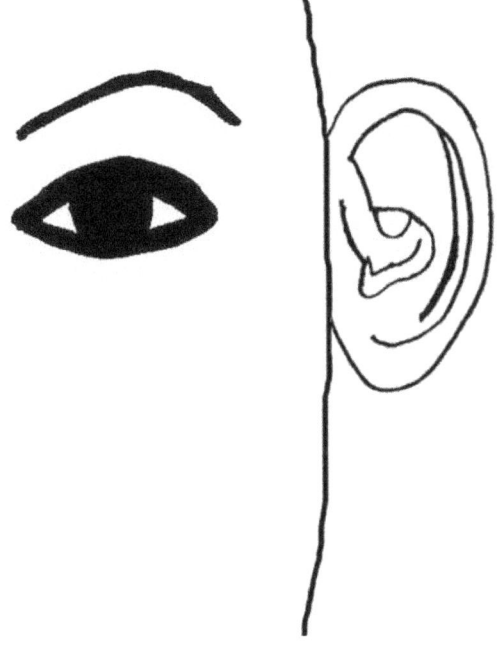

28

Types of Helix Ears

Helix is usually situated at the top part of your ears, and is located in the outer rim of your ears. People who have rounded Helix Ears tend to enjoy plenty of their own mental stimulation. They are very energetic people when it comes to making sure things are done right at their work place. This is why they are a great company towards their colleagues at work.

People with thin Helix Ears tend to be very impulsive during the process of decision-making. They are highly enthusiastic about their own career path, which resulted them to be constantly planning for what is coming next in their life. They are commonly seen to be the extroverts or alphas when you are getting to know them for the first time.

When the Helix Ears turns out to be extremely thin on the ears, they tend to be very concern about the world's economy. They will try to reason out and question the formation of humanity, and pick up subjects like history and astrology.

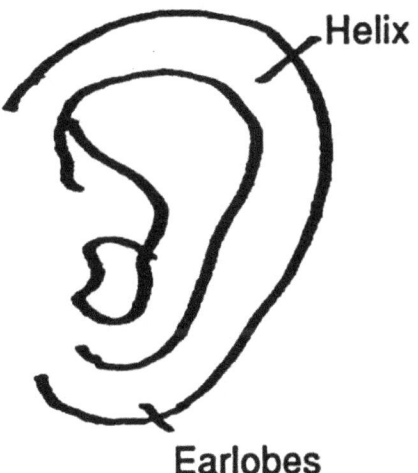

29

Types of Earlobes

Earlobes are commonly situated at the lower portion of your ears. They are found at the base of any ears and they are known to be the fleshiest part of your ears. There are two scenarios in which your earlobes can be shaped. They can either be grown in a way that is attached to the side of your head, or with the earlobes being separated from your head.

If you have earlobes that are separated from the side of your head, it represents that you can be rather independent in your own decisions. For example, you do not need to depend on anyone when you are deciding to travel to anywhere in the world. Basically, you have total faith and confidence in yourself for your own survival.

If you have earlobes that are attached to the side of your head, it indicates that you are very generous in helping the betterment of mankind to achieve your own personal satisfaction. You are bound to practice philanthropy or educate others about altruism. Just bear in mind to contribute what you can afford and you will have no issue.

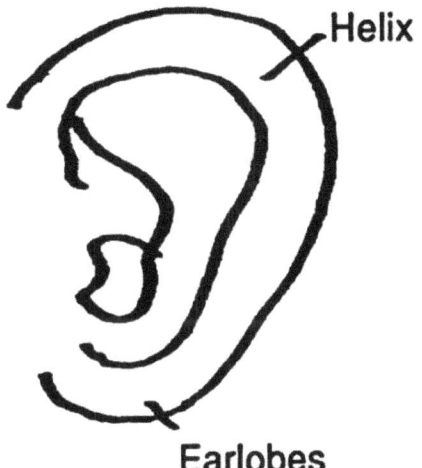

30

Long Earlobes

Long Earlobes lead a better quality of life as they age. This is one of the features that is mostly sought after for anyone to have. People with Long Earlobes tend to have a greater sense of understanding about how others will feel with their words before they speak, and this is the reason why they are always surrounded with a large group of friends wherever they go.

If they have Thick and Long Earlobes, they will have a greater capacity to achieve certain status in life while generating massive amounts of wealth. This is another feature that almost every billionaire in the world have! They are incredibly hardworking and willing to do whatever it takes to create something that will impact the world.

Women with such earlobes tend to be a money magnet and attract plenty of wealth for their partner. Especially when they are faced with any setbacks, there will always be a benefactor who will come into their life and assist them to resolve all of their obstacles.

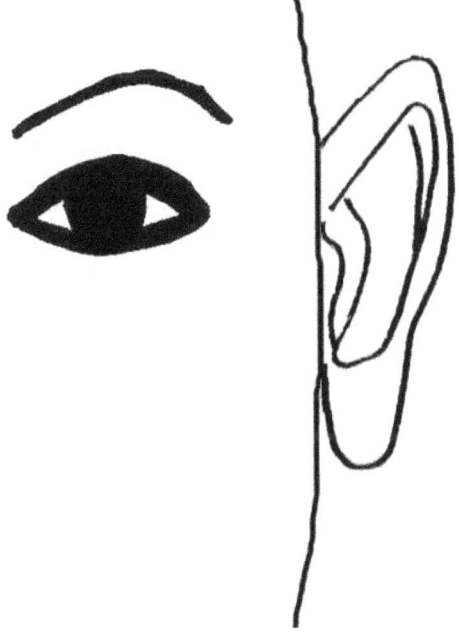

31

Our Eyes

Our Eyes are the most common feature that is revealed when we look at anyone. They not only represent our souls, but they do represent our mood for any day. Take a moment to think about this: For anyone who does not learn Physiognomy, we are able to see if someone is feeling happy, tired, stressed, or broken just by looking at their eyes. This is amazing, isn't it? To most of you, you have been doing face reading on a daily basis and you don't even realize it!

People with eyes that are wide open in their natural state tend to be more receptive and expressive individuals. A commonly seen example would be: when someone has an overwhelmed level of excitement to share a story, their eyes will be wide open before sharing it with you.

However, when someone who have narrow eyes in their natural state, tend to be suspicious and wary of their surroundings. Why? People who unknowingly narrowed their eyes at a certain time, tend to be more cautious towards their environment.

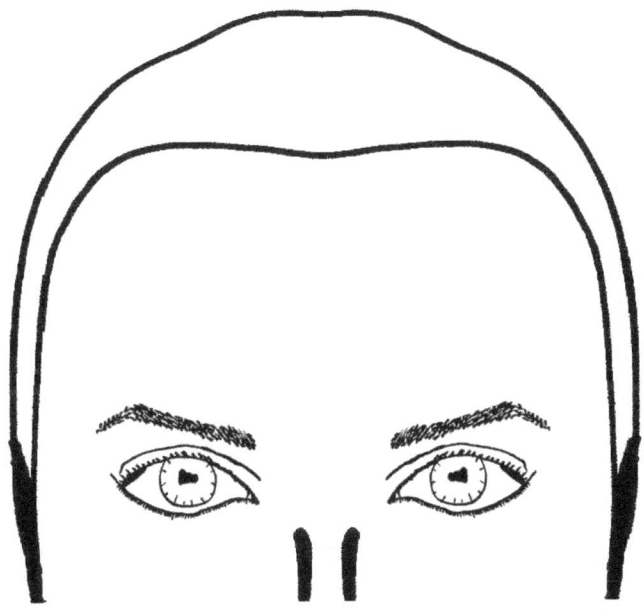

32

Massive Eyes

People with Massive Eyes are generally very attractive people in terms of their appearance, and how their huge eyes are shaped. They are very open-minded to give you a listening ear to any new suggestions.

People with Massive Eyes are very expressive people, who will tend to show you plenty of their hand gestures when you are having a conversation with them. They have an endless curiosity for people with intellectual attributes, and find them very attractive and charming. They are most suited to be in a creative career due to their wide range of imagination for creativity.

As for their personal lives, they are very warm and romantic to their loved ones. But bear in mind, they dislike boring partners who does not constantly give them an unforgettable date. An example of someone who has this facial feature would be Hollywood Actress, Emily Blunt.

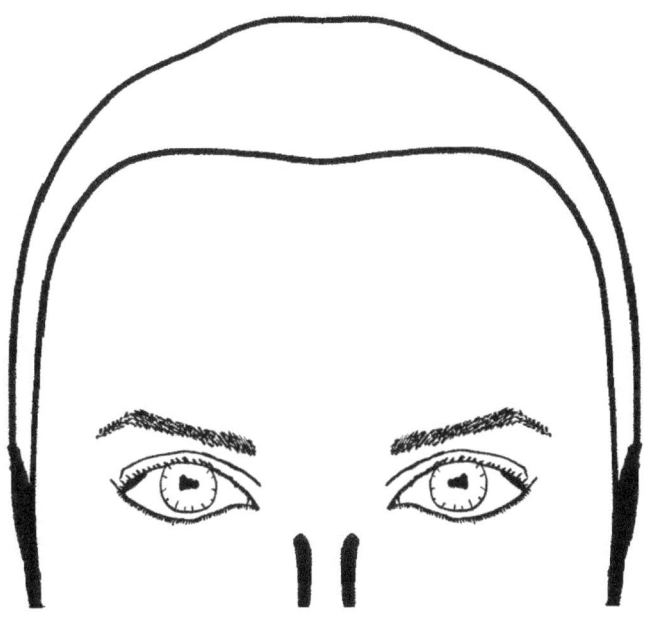

33

Mini Eyes

People with Mini Eyes are normally situated in a way that their eyes are smaller and shorter than their eyebrows. They are known to be perfectionists, as they will never take the easy way out to get things done.

Being the most skilled and observant people, they are constantly focusing on all the minor details in their business projects to ensure nothing goes wrong. They are eager to know what is happening around their surroundings, and will constantly be on the loop for changes in their environment.

As for their personal lives, jealousy will arise when they see their partner have opposite-sex friends. They have the perception of others being a threat, who will sabotage their concurrent relationship even if they are just colleagues or best friends. They may also face difficulties in opening up their emotions to the people they care about. To overcome this side effect, tell yourself to be more open in trusting your partner for things to work out better. An example of someone who has this facial feature would be Hollywood Actor, Taylor Lautner.

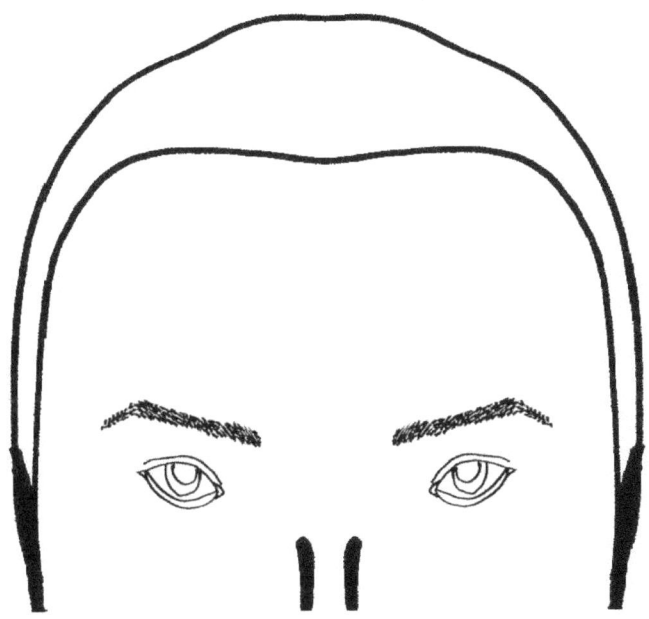

34

Circular Eyes

Circular Eyes are seen when someone has two rounded eyes on their face. People with Circular Eyes tend to be very charming and pleasant looking. They possess a charming persona that will capture your attention with their overall appearance. They are blessed with the creativity and imagination skills to look at things and change them for the better. When others are focusing on how to think outside the box, they are the ones who invented the box.

With their idealism and wild imagination in play, they often view the world in their own perception. People with Circular Eyes tend to be expressive with their facial expressions, which could make others unaware of the harmful words that are spilled out from their mouth.

They can be rather emotional, as they keep most of their feelings and thoughts bottled within them. They are often carried away by how people judge them, which could unknowingly affect their well-being in one way or another. Here is what you can do: work on your self-confidence, and focus on reinventing the things around you. An example of someone who has this facial feature would be Hollywood Actress, Emmy Rossum.

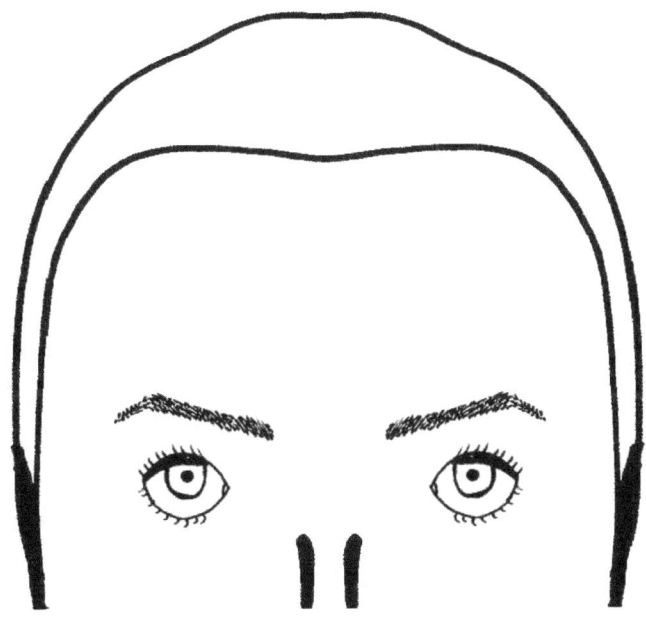

35

Narrow Set of Eyes

To determine whether the horizontal distance between your eyes is narrow or wide, try to fit two fingers in between your eyebrows. If you are able to do this, your distance is considered wide. However, if you can't, your distance would be considered as narrow.

People with Narrow Set of Eyes are blessed with the ability to concentrate on what they are doing. They tend to spark an interest in things that the majority of people in the world do not. This is one of the reasons why they might have a high tendency of overworking their brain, as they focus on too many minor details.

Their low tolerance for external influences such as, traffic jam during busy hours, and the room temperature surrounding their environment resulted them in having mood swings. These external factors will result them to be emotionally stressed and obnoxious easily. You should learn to adapt to any environment if you have this set of eyes!

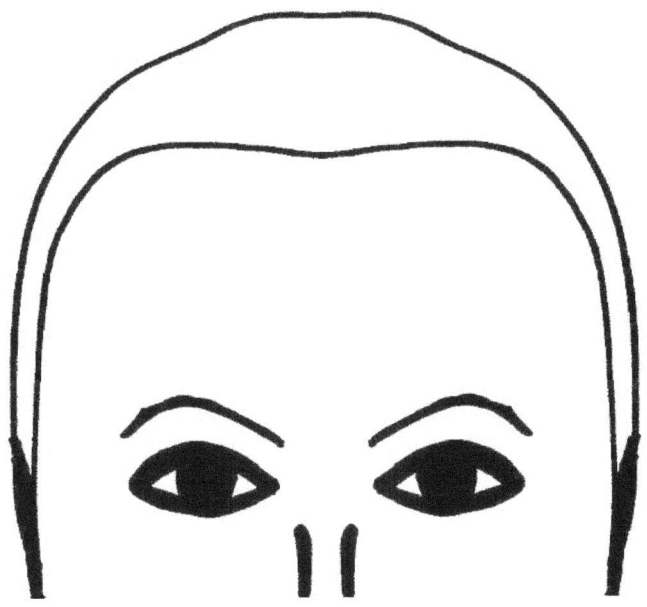

36

Wide Set of Eyes

People with Wide Set of Eyes naturally focus on doing one particular thing for a long period of time. They have the tendency of not paying much attention to details, despite spending so much time on doing one thing alone.

They are stupendously great in managing a team of people, as they have the capability of looking at what others can offer to grow the company. They enjoy forecasting growths to look at the bigger picture to create their action plan for the long run. If you look at the top performance managers in a company, you will see that most of them have this feature.

They are tolerant with any problems that surfaces, with the perception of all these setbacks being a stepping stone to success. They see external influences as an opportunity to lead others and showcase their abilities. Simply said, they are the problem solvers and assets in any company. Cherish them well, because you need them to grow your company!

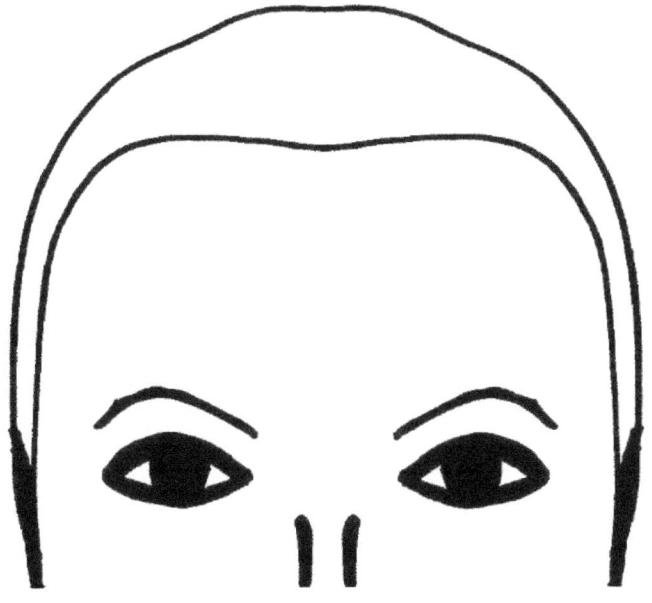

37

Embedded Eyes

Embedded Eyes can be seen when the depth of the eyes is set deeply in the face and buried in their skull. You can recognize this facial feature easily when you see them from the side.

People with Embedded Eyes are believed to be visionaries and true observers in their own nature. They are constantly building and forecasting situations before the completion of any projects. They love to observe their external surroundings wherever they go and imagine the future growth of their surroundings in the upcoming years.

Before conversing with these people, they will always gather insights on what you have achieved to determine if you are worthy for them to listen to. To get their attention, you will need to share your credentials and past achievements to have a meaningful conversation with them. An example of someone who has this facial feature would be Hollywood Actress, Megan Fox.

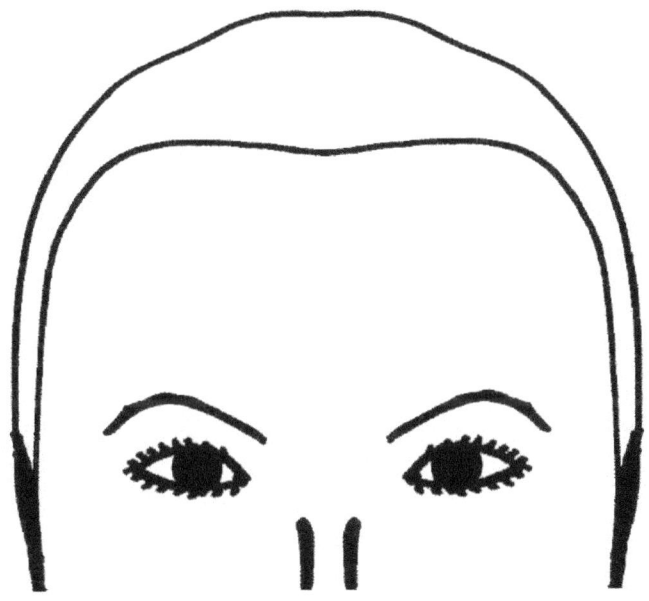

38

Popping Eyes

Popping Eyes are seen when someone who has eyes that are bulging out like a goldfish. People with Popping Eyes are energetic to complete their projects, but are impulsive when it comes to decision making. Due to their rash nature, they tend to sign up for almost any enrichment courses that may not benefit them.

People with Popping Eyes tend to make harsh and unnecessary remarks to get the attention from others. Therefore, with this persona, they love to be the center of attention regardless of the impressions placed on the eyes of others. This is one of the reasons why they tend to scare away their potential life benefactors.

Bear in mind, if you have friends who have this feature, you have to learn to be more accommodative to them. They will feel offended if you ignore their presence, and may hold a grudge against you if you fail to give them the attention they seek. An example of someone who has this facial feature would be Hollywood Actress, Amanda Seyfried.

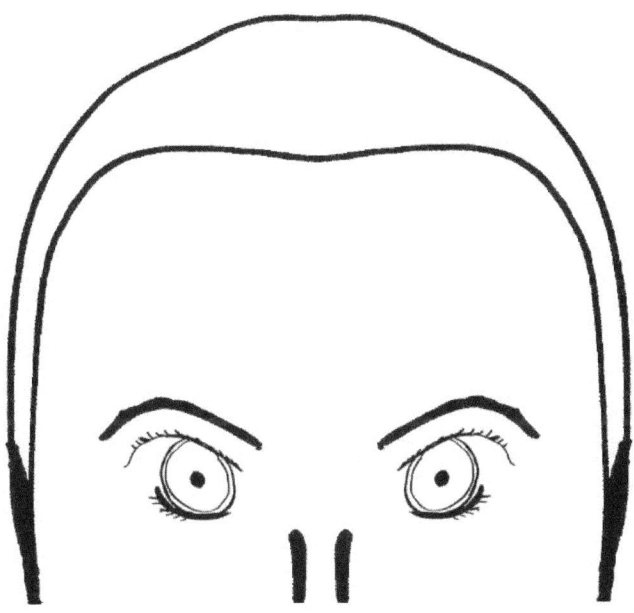

39

Upward Set Eyes

Upward Set Eyes are seen when the outer corners of both eyes are set higher than the inner side. People with Upward Set Eyes have a positive and ambitious outlook of life, as they tend to live every moment to the fullest!

No one can stop them when they have set their eyes on something they want to get done. They are very driven to ensure every event goes according their way until they succeed. Being strong motivators, they are a strong influence within their social circle. They will constantly be encouraging others to be optimistic in whatever they pursue.

They are mostly admired for their optimism, as they are always filled with plenty of witty remarks. Being ambitious people, they are constantly on the run for new business opportunities to seek growth as an individual. Now you know who are the ones who are constantly increasing the bar of our society status!

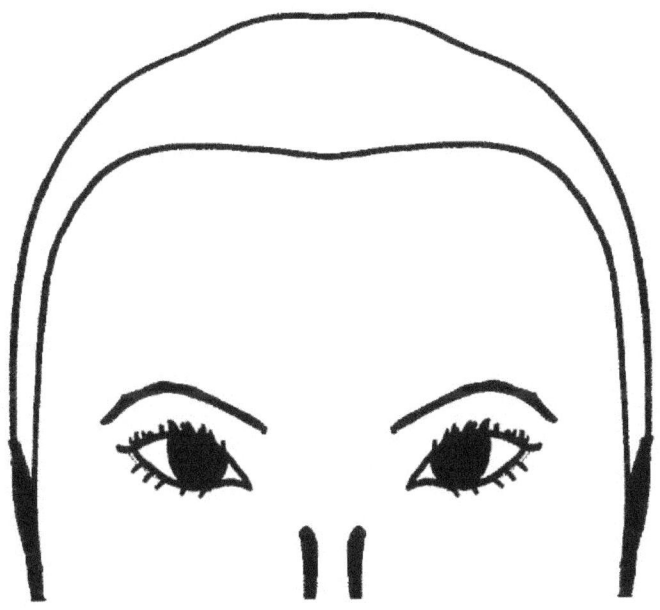

40

Downward Set Eyes

Downward Set Eyes are seen when the inner corners of both eyes are set higher than the outer side of the eyes. They tend to have a more negative perception towards life, due to the fact that they are constantly focusing on living for others.

People with Downward Set Eyes are willing to go beyond their best ability, and sacrifice things which they treasure the most, in order to help those in need. With this selfless nature, they may sacrifice their own needs to assist others. If you have this set of eyes, I encourage you to first work on your own self-development, and this can result you to helping a larger scale of people in the long run. Forget about the small scale; impact our world by leaving a legacy when you can help more than you can imagine!

People who have both corners of their eyes on the same level are known to have Straight Set Eyes. Straight Set Eyes will have a balanced point of outlook in life, as they promote fairness towards their social circle. This would be known to be the most common set of eyes around.

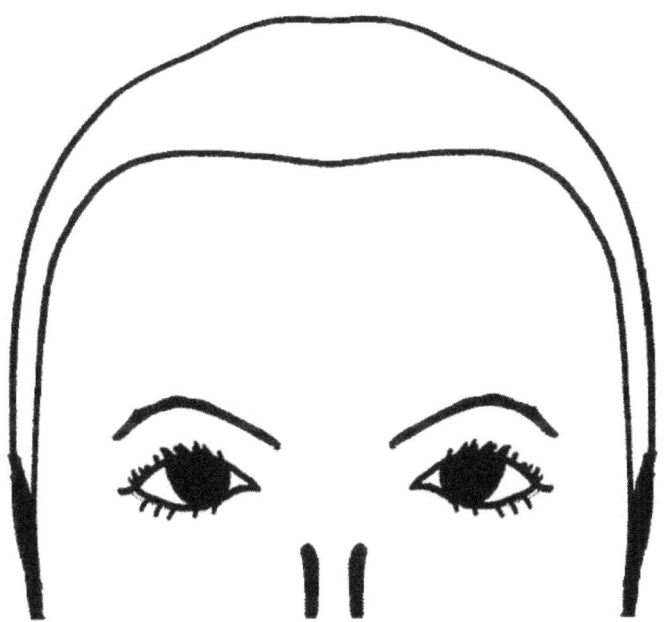

41

Special Effects for Eyes

Special Effects for Eyes will give us insights on the current cycle of events in anyone's life right now. This tells us if anyone is going through favorable or unfavorable life cycles at this very moment!

People who have crystal clear eyes with a glossy effect of a marble, represents that they are currently going through a good life cycle with plenty of abundance and wealth opportunities. They currently have minimal struggles in life, and are optimistic towards living their life at this instant. This would be a favorable special eyes effect to have throughout one's life.

The other Special Effects for Eyes would be blurry eyes. People with blurry eyes are seen to have greyish effects around their eyes. This represents that they are currently going through some issues that are draining them out mentally and physically. If you see red veins or blood vessels popping around the eyes, please get them to consult a psychiatrist immediately! As they are in the midst of turning insane with the overwhelming issues in their life!

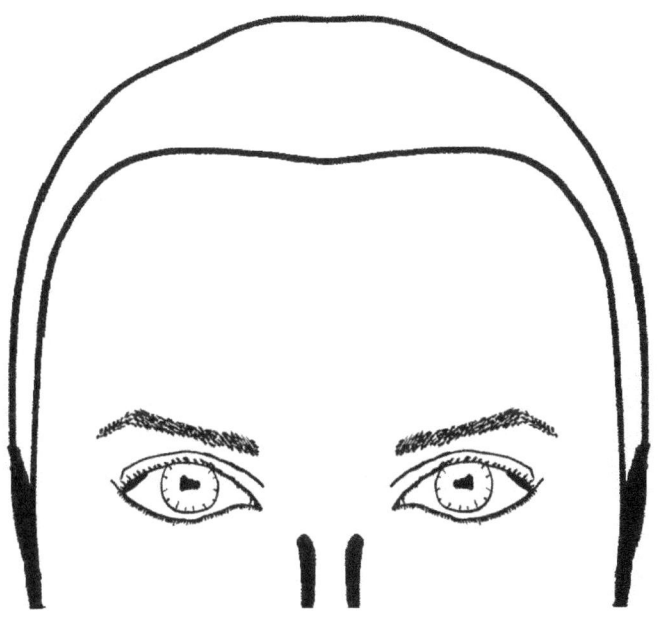

42

Massive Lips

Massive Lips are generally so thick that you might have to fight the strong urge to not kiss them! People with Massive Lips are unquestionably talkative to the extent whereby they create the center of attention in every party. They will never be quiet, as communication is their forte!

They are best suited to be the main drivers for sales, as they never fail to promote any products or services. With their presence, they will never allow you to be in boredom. However, if they are hanging out with people who are not attracted to listen to them, they may result in placing a certain level of annoyance in the group.

Bear in mind that keeping promises will never be their forte, unless they are influenced by strong external factors like religion or mentors. A good way to reveal their fullest potential is when you need directions in a new country, look for someone with Massive Lips on the street, and they will give you the full details to get to your destination. An example of someone who has this facial feature would be Hollywood Actress, Angelina Jolie.

43

Mini Lips

Mini Lips are generally so thin that you might wonder if they have any lips! People with Mini Lips are less talkative compared to the ones with Massive Lips. They prefer to keep their life private and confidential. This would result them in being unexpressive with their emotions to others, and hence, they are not an open book.

They are the best people to keep any secrets if you intend to share it with someone, but you do not want others to know. They are more bounded to keep their words and honor their promises due to their sensitive nature. Being conservative people, they tend to be more cautious with their words and the things they do.

As for their career, they prefer things to be done with quality than quantity. They are driven towards producing work with high standards, despite being sophisticated people. You should shower them with beautiful compliments, as they love to be pampered, and you will make their day.

44

Upward Lip Line

Lip lines can be seen between the upper and lower lip when a mouth is closed fully. Ensure that you do not have any expressions to alter your natural state, and you will be able to see if you have a straight lip line or with the ends going upwards or downwards.

People with an Upward Lip Line is an optimist, and they are blessed to look into all the positive aspects that are bound to happen in life. With this highly favorable blessing, how do you use them? When you have a potential business venture that you are considering to go into, you can approach them to get insights about how much potential your venture has! But bear in mind to not overlook the downside.

They tend to miss out on all the things that could possibly happen if the idea does not work out as intended. Understand this part of the picture and you will be able to make a conclusion if you should proceed with your business venture.

45

Downward Lip Line

Downward Lip Line is seen when the sides of the mouth is pointing downwards. People with Downward Lip Line are more pessimistic towards their outlook of life, as they tend to expect and only see the negative side of things. Their remarks they usually say are negative and unnecessary during any occasion.

In Physiognomy, you can turn any unfavorable traits to your advantage. One of the ways you can capitalize on people with Downward Lip Line to your benefit is: by confronting them with any business projects you are about to venture in. They will provide you with all the cons if your plan does not work out as intended! As they can open your mind to every extreme negative scenario that can happen, because they love to anticipate the worst in everything.

But bear in mind, after being flooded with all these possible risks, remember to always balance out the scale of benefits, and not allow their opinions to get in the way if there are more positive aspects in the full picture.

46

Straight Lip Line

People with Straight Lip Lines are believed to be well-balanced people for their overall outlook in life. They are known to be very reactive towards living their life especially when the events are changing rapidly.

When odds are going towards their favor, they have an optimistic view of life. However, when things around them are not going according to plan, their mindset will instantly switch to becoming pessimistic, and hence, restricting them in taking any risks.

When conversing with them for business ventures, they will give you the full picture of both pros and cons of how a project could possibly turn out. However, they are least likely to give you the extreme sides of both positive and negative outcomes. You can choose to approach them if you do not want to know about the extreme perception of things. This lip line is commonly found among the majority of people.

47

Circular Chin

A Circular Chin is seen when someone has a semi-circle projected below their face. Due to their friendly nature, they will seldom show an aggressive side to others. Reason is, they value how they portray their image to the public and their social circle of friends.

Circular Chin is commonly seen among male celebrities. People with Circular Chin are able to acquire plenty of support from benefactors and mentors who are willing to assist them in their career. They are blessed with good personal relations, and therefore they love to attend social events to network and mingle with new people.

They are very approachable by nature, and they are the next best feature you can look for when asking for directions. If you see someone who has a Circular Chin together with Massive Lips, they are the best combination for you to approach when seeking for directions when you are lost in any country! They might even show you the way and take you to where you want to go!

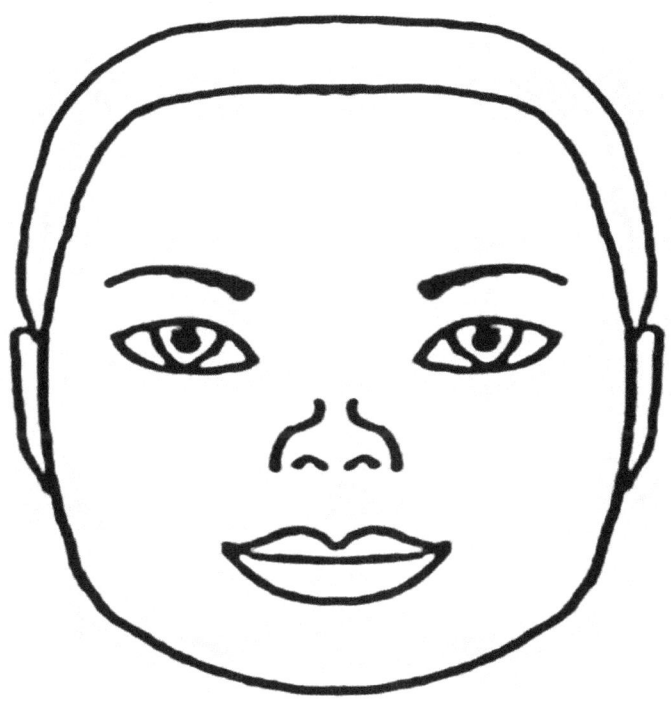

48

Squarish Chin

A Squarish Chin is seen when someone who has a chin that is shaped like a square at the bottom of their face. People with Squarish Chin enjoys challenging themselves by fixing the biggest problems at their workplace, and the challenges in their personal life. They have the mindset of warriors, and will not stop fighting until they get what they desire.

If you look at athletes who have this chin, they are one of the strongest competitors in the field. They will look at everything as a challenge even though it might be fun for others to do it. But bear in mind, they will be difficult to defeat. The solution? You have to think like a warrior when you are competing with them and not let your guard down.

They can also make great lawyers as they love to debate and will not stop until the case is finalized. However, they tend to make plenty of enemies due to their nature of being too demanding when asking others for favors. They simply need to learn to respect others, as they have the mindset that everyone is oblige to give them a helping hand.

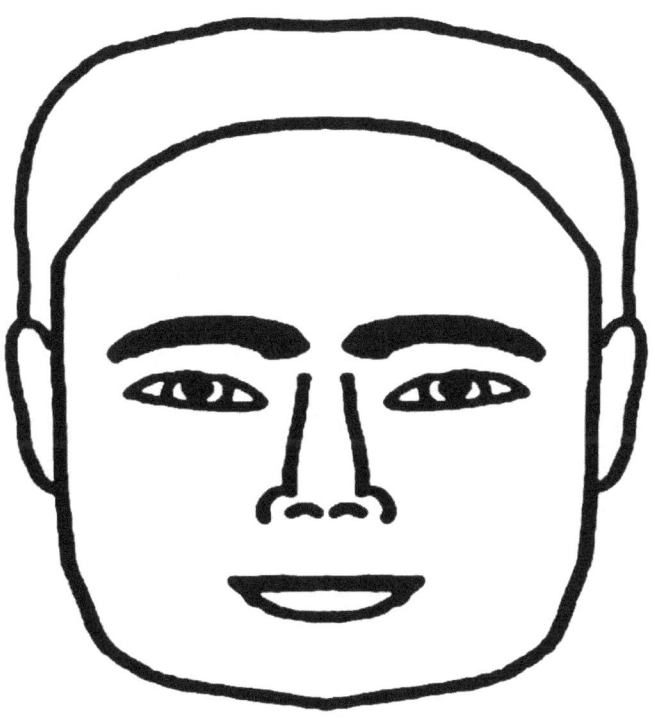

49

Arrow Chin

An Arrow Chin is seen when the bottom of a face is projected to have a sharp V like an arrow pointing downwards. They tend to be very sensitive, hot-tempered, and joyous people. They can be quite stubborn towards others, and thus they may end up with not many good friends as they age.

People with an Arrow Chin have an inner self where they can be nasty when pressured, as they tend to do things in their own way. They have their own unique perception of life, as they tend to gossip and stalk others to find out about the latest updates in their personal lives.

However, they have a high tendency to cheat on their spouse, as they may feel unwanted if their spouse can't spend enough time and give them the active sexual lifestyle that they desire. Betrayal could be avoided if their spouse is flexible enough to understand their needs and wants.

50

Popping Chin

A Popping Chin can be seen when the bottom of the chin is protruding outwards like a witch where you have seen in most movies. People with Popping Chin rarely quits when things are done half way, as they have a very strong willpower to complete anything they started.

You can task them with anything that is impossible to do, because they will find a way to get them done. They are best suited to be the key people at huge corporations to lead their team with their strong leadership abilities. They are blessed with the ability to fix most of the impossible problems in their own company with their 'outside the box' solutions.

As for their personal relationships, they tend to think of their spouse all the time! If they are experiencing any breakups, they won't let the matter rest quickly due to their possessive nature. With their strong willpower, they will continue to press them for as long as possible in hope for a better outcome.

Acknowledgements

First and foremost, to you my dear reader, thank you for investing your time in reading this book. I hope that you can embrace this new skill of yours to tackle any business or personal problems that may surface to you. I look forward to hearing all of your success stories, and how you will impact this world of ours.

There are no words to share my gratitude to the many people who believed in this book and gave so much of their time to make the publication of "50 Ways to Read Anyone, Anywhere, Anytime" possible. I would like to take this opportunity to thank these following individuals for their constant support and reaching out to me by giving me the necessary insights on what to include in this book. If this book serves people well, it is because of the quality of your guidance and contribution of being selfless souls.

My biggest thanks goes out to Lily. Through her depth of conviction and sheer force of her will, her encouragement and motivation gives me the power to complete this book. She told me that this would be an important personal journey for me, and she was right. She reminded me the key moments, without whom there is no way this book would be written.

The boundless support from my family has been the foundation of my life. My deepest love to both my sisters, Annie, and Winnie Tay. Annie, I hope you will be able to ignite and muster all your courage towards becoming a renowned public presenter in years to come. Winnie, your pleasant charisma is what separates you from the majority of people. Remember to always stay obsessed to your purpose, and serve the highest level possible. Mom and Dad, despite your lack of faith for this book during the initial stage, you supported me in the end. Thank you for being the grace of our creator. You have both imparted so much love for me to be more. I love you all!

Much love to my extended family, Doris Khaw, who has been so understanding for the months I was busy and welcoming me back with open arms when writing this book. You are one of my dearest friends in life and you inspire me to see what is possible. Thank you for all the laughter and love throughout the years.

Denise Chen Qiuming, thank you for all the love you poured into me and believing in this crazy dream of mine. Your encouragement gives me the power to transform lives. Your care and source of love is something I could never imagine.

Tham Heng Mun, thank you for all your support you have given me for decades. You truly are a genius, and yet so humble. The way you take an idea and turn it into a reality excites everyone around you. Each day I spend with you is another day I am inspired to take my life to a whole new level.

To my publishing crew that made this book possible: My exceptional editor, Emily, believed in this project so much that she turned these ideas of mine and continually pushed me to share my thoughts in this book. She was instrumental in helping me to flesh out ideas and turning them into outlines and finally chapters. She stayed up many late nights to line edit every sentence. Thank you for believing in me and betting on this book. Your enthusiasm and passion for this project is truly inspiring.

Big thanks to my copy editor, Audrina Rahayu, who is so skillful at improving and changing every last detail of the drawings that astounds me. Your unflagging support keeps this project on the fast track to completion.

Massive thanks to the design team for visually bringing this concept into life and for putting my ideas on the right direction along the way. From taking my scattered thoughts and putting them into appealing visuals, it was a gratifying experience to work with you all!

To the legal team for drafting out all the contracts for U.S. Copyright Office to protect this book from any copyright infringements, thank you! It was a privilege to work with you all as a family!

My deepest gratitude goes to Nicklaus Chiam, I have been very thankful for knowing you. It is the privilege of my lifetime and it surpasses my wildest dreams to be a part of your life. Our constant messages for words of encouragement, they meant the world to me.

Macy Chen, I am grateful to have you as my sister. You are the person I can really count on whenever I need a drink! With those unlimited refills of sake, it does help me to take my mind off after a long day! You will always be a part of my life.

Titaporn Nasaarn, you are insanely smart, talented, and kind in every way. It is always a delight when you are sharing with me the life of being a doctor. You gave me a vast knowledge about our human body for me to relate to Physiognomy in ways I could ever imagine.

Anaya J, you are literally one of the most genuine person I have ever met throughout my entire life. Our projects of venturing into Thailand with this book would not be possible without you. I am blessed to call you my business partner.

Hannah Lee, you brought your unparalleled talent of being meticulous for synthesizing the content so it is concise, understandable, and convincing to any reader. Your analytical rigor is very insightful.

To my Californian family: Georgiana Nistor, Grigoras Adelina Elisabeta, Closca Ana Diana, Abdurezzak Bilgic, Kubra Karadag, Eylul Sen, Carla Cesarean, Raita Cristina, and Sudipta Mohapatra. I look forward to our next reunion! You have all encouraged me to speak from my heart with conviction and confidence. I am so grateful to be a part of your life and all the epic hugs!

My BC family: Zhang Yelly, Zheng Qiupeng, Kanisorn Oonjittkul, Xi Zirong, Ghada Bal, Rie Arai, Lalita Ladsai May, and Maprang Kochaporn. Our constant meetups are always amazing and I love how we are all from different countries. Thank you for constantly giving me lots of banter. We will be in touch!

My college family: Vivien Hang, Kaori Konuma, Fergye Venessia, Celise Tan, Sijin Rue, Nayoung Lee, Herin Park, Shin Bee Park, Meixin Chen, Taeim Kim, Heng Tho, Abegail Aileen, and Esther Katrina. You have all made a difference in my college life and I thank you for it! We might be separated across countries, but we are only a message away!

Anyone who pursues our Bachelor's degree in Singapore knows that friends become family here. Many of us moved far away from home to pursue our education. My UCD family has been an abundance of joy. From dinners, to movies, to coffee talks, and to walk the talks, I am deeply grateful for all of you: Nicole Kuan, Nhi Le June, Kim Thanh Amy, Aigerim Kydyrova, Sharon Yeo, Pamela Kwong, Gabriel Wang, Hayley Huang, Alex Piamwiwattikul, Katrina Mu, May Yang, Momo Liu, Felita Candra, Oliver Wam, Christine Liu, Sandy Yap, Sandi Thwin, Pratama Putra Tamtam, Dipan Mehta, Jason Tan, Stanley Hoe, John Menon, Chandni Krishnan, Saw Kyaw, Quynh Khanh, Gloria Yuan, Bailu, Li sha, Jason William Ho, and Jieun Paik. Some of you generously read drafts and offered thoughts, sometimes under demanding deadlines. I would like to say thank you for being a part of this book from the bottom of my heart, I look forward to watching all of your career unfold!

Masahide Hanashiro, Keitarou Kakihana, Katsunari Takahashi, and Tokashiki Kota. Thank you for flooding me with all the constant golf tips to improve my golf skills. Not forgetting all our visits to the finest Japanese cuisines our bellies can savor whenever I need a break from work. You guys rock!

Siriwat Jaravechason, Nuntiya Jaravechason, Phisan Noonkliang, and Araya Niradpai, you are all so close to me and have touched my life deeply. My life has been powerfully shaped by your depth of love and generosity. All of you are the light for hope, without you, the world will be filled with a whole lot of darkness.

My mentor Cead, no matter how often we talk, you are the beacon of my light and you inspire me to keep going. Thank you for all your warmth, patience, kindness, and good humor. You have inspired me to grow from afar in countless ways to become an international author, public speaker, and to running my own companies. I know that I am doing something right because of your mentorship and guidance. Your love, devotion, and joy is a burning light inside me.

My meditation mentor who have provided me spiritual support and solace to keep me sane: Phra TedSiddhivides. Thank you for all the sessions you gave me with so much heart, a second home I can go to whenever I need to clear my mind.

I am eternally grateful to all my courageous clients who generously allow me to grow their empires. You are a huge source of inspiration for me every single day. You are insanely supportive and generous. I will not be naming names due to client privilege, but you know who you are! It is the highest honor to be a part of your team to see how you manage thousands of employees every day.

If I missed out any of your names in these acknowledgements, forgive me! You know you are a part of my life. Any omissions are inadvertent. I am so grateful for all your friendships and this new adventure of ours. Will I be writing another book? Most likely! As I have over a thousand ways in my own collection!

Changing the world requires you to have courage to stand up to critics and continue the path to your purpose. Innovating extraordinary products or services is one way to leave your memorable footprint on earth. We should all create an impact, even if it is small. Our passion defines our life, our purpose drives us to become better, and our products show the world what we believe in. I hope you have enjoyed this book as much as I have. I will be cheering you on the path you are taking from here. May you be striving and live life passionately. May you exceed all your wildest expectations and savor all your small success in between. Finally, may you reach for the moon and share it with others in life.

Winson Tay
Author of 50 Ways to Read Anyone, Anywhere, Anytime

GET A HEAD START WITH A FACE READING PROFESSIONAL

Starting on an adventure after graduation or on your own can be daunting and tough. With the guidance of our highly trained and motivating consultants, you will be able to discover your:

- Passion in Life/Career Pursuits

- Favorable Industries to Enter for Higher Returns

- Unfavorable Industries that creates more resistance to your success

- Identifying your Life Benefactors/Mentors to assist you in your journey of life

- Strategic Analysis for Business Owners/Corporations

- Maximize your Potential as a Person

- And MORE!

Visit winsontay.com/services for more information!

INVITING US TO ANY OF YOUR WORLDWIDE CORPORATE EVENTS

At Winson Tay Consulting Firm, we have worked with many worldwide reputable companies to help build their team of people through Physiognomy, Ontology, Phrenology, and Cosmology. Led by Winson Tay as the keynote speaker for all corporate events, our clientele comes from all walks of life. We customize our seminars and talks to suit your requirements depending on your group of audiences. As we are constantly expanding internationally, any special requests from any countries are welcome.

Singapore, Thailand, Cambodia, United States, China, and expanding!

winsontay.com

FREE BONUS FOR YOU
:: Worth $97 ::

For purchasing this book, I've a collection of bonuses that I'm willing to share them with you. You'll receive strategies that was learnt through years of experience from entrepreneurs that have helped them to create massive fortunes.

Here is what you'll be getting:

Get connected to our Global community for FREE!

Go to this URL: www.winsontay.com/community to have an access to a library filled with so much information!

Do leave a review on the website and I look forward to hear your success story in months to come.

MORE SECRETS ON PHYSIOGNOMY WILL SOON BE COMING YOUR WAY

One of the most valuable assets a person can have is the ability to learn and grow as a person. This ability will determine if others are willing to pay you a premium to acquire what you know. By improving yourself, your ability will be deemed valuable and your net worth will increase rapidly every year. Our greatest responsibility is to help you organize your time to achieve more for your career or business advancement into the indefinite future.

Our studies will be tested and proven that can help save our readers' years and years of hard work and thousands of dollars for research. They will be carefully designed to ensure a comprehensive, yet impactful syllabus. Let Winson show you how to organize your life onto the right path to accomplish the maximum potential at every stage of your career. Subscribe to winsonlay.com to receive the latest updates!

Available when the next book is ready in the coming years...

HISTORY ABOUT PHYSIOGNOMY

In ancient times, Physiognomy was passed down through generations only by masters to disciples that are worthy to learn this art of study. These disciples will then spend countless of years under their guidance to learn bit by bit from their master. With this ancient culture, most of the technicalities about this subject have been lost while passing down generations after generations in the process.

These classical studies have been resurfaced by Winson and he re-designed the entire syllabus to fit into today's modern world. With constant research and findings on this subject, he has been focusing on building a constant improvement about Physiognomy. It is now easy to read by most people with the illustrations provided to understand this art of study. With this skill, he has been sought after by the board of directors for business empires and featured on countless of articles and magazines.

This subject was once only used by China's sagacious emperors to select their right subordinates and people to lead a city. In today's context, it is used by corporations to select the right candidates and adopted by anyone who knows how to use it. However, there is no credence or references to indicate that Physiognomy works, but there is only one way for you to find out. Apply it into your life and you will see wonders.

SHARE THIS BOOK WITH OTHERS

Also available in Thai

Other languages will be ready soon...

To order bulk copies of this book, you can contact the author on the website below for a quote. Special discounts will be given for employee giveaways, fundraising or educational use.

winsontay.com

Winson Tay is the Founder and Chief Analyst of Winson Tay Consulting Firm, a global consulting company specializing in Physiognomy, Ontology, Cosmology, Phrenology, and other Chinese Metaphysics subjects. His vision is to create a public platform for our world to communicate openly and understand one another upon meeting each other for the first time.

Milton Keynes UK
Ingram Content Group UK Ltd.
UKHW011825270224
438561UK00005B/637